ZOO ANIMALS

GALLERY BOOKS
An Imprint of W. H. Smith Publishers Inc.
112 Madison Avenue
New York City 10016

This edition first published in U.S.
in 1990 by Gallery Books,
an imprint of W.H. Smith Publishers, Inc.
112 Madison Avenue, New York, New York 10016

ISBN 0-8317-9583-2

Printed and bound in Spain

For rights information about the photographs in
this book please contact:

The Image Bank
111 Fifth Avenue, New York, NY 10003

Producer: Solomon M. Skolnick
Author: Marcus Schneck
Design Concept: Lesley Ehlers
Designer: Ann-Louise Lipman
Editor: Joan E. Ratajack
Production: Valerie Zars
Photo Researcher: Edward Douglas
Assistant Photo Researcher: Robert V. Hale
Editorial Assistant: Carol Raguso

Title page: **A few giant pandas are housed
in zoos, but the species has not had much
success at breeding under captive conditions. The zoo-based population is not
self-sustaining.** *Opposite:* **In sharp contrast
to giant pandas, lions in captivity are
generally prolific breeders. Each year
seems to produce a plentiful supply of
new lions for all zoos that want them.**

The great, white polar bear paused for a moment, nose to nose with the human. A few inches of plexiglass, seemingly fragile against the 900-pound animal, was all that separated them. Despite the perfectly safe conditions, the hairs on the back of the 170-pound man's neck stood on end.

Zoos – at least the best of them – are magical places, packed with animal-human encounters of this close kind. Here, the lion can stalk its prey, the giant panda can lounge about munching on ample supplies of bamboo, the lemur can bound around its tree-filled environment. And it all happens within clear, safe view. Nature's grandest plays are performed daily.

Nearly everyone goes to the zoo at least once, although that is far from an adequate experience given the major and speedy changes that are being made today. More than 112 million Americans visit one version or another of the venerable institution annually.

People go to the zoo for many reasons. For most, it is the last link to a wild world that still beckons. For others, the chance to introduce their children to other forms of life is the draw.

Zoo lions spend a great deal of their time asleep, something that concerns many visitors. However, this is a natural behavior, which they would follow in the wild as well.

Above: The big cats, such as this male lion, are generally among the most popular animals in the zoo. The powerful, potentially fierce predators hold a special fascination for people. *Below:* "King of the Beasts" is how we know the male lion, but this is really not an appropriate title. In the wild, the male generally relies on the females of the pride to do the hunting. *Opposite:* Although the Siberian tiger has been pushed into extinction over much of its original range, zoo-based populations are thriving.

What insiders, both in zoos and in preserves, have come to term "mega-fauna" are generally the big attractions. These are the big, charismatic creatures, generally fur-covered, warm-blooded, and with a hint of cuddliness about them, like lions, tigers, and bears. To that list we could add elephants, zebras, and giraffes. While reptile houses will draw a few oohs and aahs, it is the mega-fauna that gathers and holds the large crowds. Add a baby of one of these species and the attraction is unbeatable.

There are also "stars" of the zoo, individual animals that capture the imagination of the world and boost admissions to their particular zoo. The two giant pandas, Hsing-Hsing and Ling-Ling, are prime examples.

But not everyone enjoys a trip to the zoo. There are those who would put an end to zoos, viewing anything other than the wild state as demeaning to the animals. Some members of the animal rights movement have gone so far as to express a preference for extinction over the survival of a species under protective zoo conditions.

They point to the cramped and unnatural quarters, lethargic animals, low levels of knowledge-able care, and ridiculous "acts" such as juggling seals that, admittedly, still do exist at some zoos. Even today there are some very bad zoos, more deserving of the name "menagerie," that are nothing but concrete and steel cages holding a collection of maladjusted chimpanzees and sleeping lions.

But those zoos are fast becoming relics of the past rather than the normal state of affairs. The traditional idea of a zoo as a place where living animals are kept in cages for exhibition is rapidly changing. Zoos throughout the world are engaged in the most massive redesign and rebuilding movement in their history, with an eye toward recreating natural habitats and maintaining herds and packs of animals doing whatever comes naturally to them. In one year alone (1987) zoos across America spent more than $500 million in this effort. Major work is under way in nearly every American city that houses a zoo.

Larger spaces, non-public living areas, natural social groupings and interactions, and concern for the physical and mental well-being of the animals are the hallmarks of these new zoos.

As a result, the gorillas that inhabit the $4.5 million rain forest in Zoo Atlanta have formed themselves into family groups and mated, which is a rare occurrence outside of the wild. Likewise, beavers in the Minnesota Zoo have produced offspring in their enclosure, which is complete with a continuous supply of

This page, top to bottom: **Although they are the largest cats on Earth, Siberian tigers have readily adapted to life in captivity and even do well in old-style concrete and steel bar cages. A Sumatran tiger chews on its meal at the edge of one of the moats in the San Diego Zoo's new, cageless Tiger River exhibit. Much of a captive tiger's time is spent on the prowl, exploring its environment.**

Tigers are excellent swimmers and never hesitate to enter the water. Broad moats with sharp drop-offs, rather than ponds, are needed to contain them in exhibits without bars. *Below:* Two Sumatran tiger cubs, born to a captive mother, are completely at ease in their man-made environment.

willow saplings for the animals to gnaw on. Bats fly about the caves of New York City's Central Park Zoo's specially lit, simulated nighttime environment.

These are the new zoos, where visitors stroll through the environments the animals inhabit. Moats and sheets of plexiglass separate humans from animals. The inhabitants go about their daily routine, often partially hidden from the visitors, but always providing more of a look into their natural existence than their bar-enclosed predecessors did. Ecologically related species are displayed together – in the same enclosure when possible – in place of the old taxonomic system that put all the bears in one location, all the lions in another, and all the hoofed animals in yet another.

Although the idea that zoos need to help in the preservation of certain species was discussed as early as the 1940's, the true "new zoo" might be seen as arriving in the nick of time. The institution's role is still changing from that of an encyclopedic catalog of the animal world to the last hope for some species. There are now creatures that exist nowhere except in zoos. The future of these species depends entirely upon their success in captivity.

Albinism occurs in virtually all animal species. The unusual coloration makes the animals prize attractions, like this white bengal tiger at Busch Gardens, Tampa, Florida. *Left:* Two Bengal tigers share a moment of rough-housing – the difference in their colors appears to be unnoticed by them.

Guam rails, a small forest bird from that Pacific island, were removed from the wild in 1984, as biologists rounded up all but two of the last 18 birds. With the World War II introduction of the predatory brown tree snake to Guam, the rail population plummeted from tens of thousands. Under protected, captive conditions, there are now more than 120 of the birds, all maintained in zoos. Similarly, the last 30 or so California condors on the face of the Earth exist only in captivity.

Przewalski's horse, the only true wild horse, is believed to be extinct in its native Siberia. However, captive herds in zoos around the world have done very well in increasing their numbers.

The last wild wisent, or European bison, died in 1925, but the species continues today in small zoo-herds across the globe, as does the Pere David deer.

This page, top to bottom: **Because of their beautiful coats and the fact they inhabit areas that man wants for his domestic animals, jaguars are an endangered species, although viable populations still exist in scattered pockets of its former range. Many exotic cats have been hunted to near extinction for their fur. The serval, a small feline species native to Africa, is able to jump a dozen feet straight up into the air in pursuit of prey and thus catch domestic birds that wander into its cage in search of food.**

Preceding pages: Unless conditions in their native Africa and Asia change drastically, rhinoceroses may be found nowhere outside of zoos. *These pages:* Animals born in captivity like this one-month-old rhinoceros are the key to the future for many highly endangered species. *Below:* A rhino trots by what appear to be huge boulders, but which are actually the man-made background to its naturalistic enclosure.

The Bronx Zoo in New York City has had great success in breeding the pygmy hippopotamus since it hosted the first captive birth of one of the small, rare "river horses" in 1919. *Opposite:* Generally undemanding in captivity, although a bathing pool is an absolute necessity, they are prolific breeders under zoo conditions.

In many ways this young zebra has an easier life than its wild counterparts on the Serengeti Plains in Africa which migrate during the wet and dry seasons. *Left:* For many species, including the ungulates like the zebra, mother-offspring activity remains the same whether in the zoo or in the wild, but other species have shown a great deal of difficulty in continuing their normal behavior in captivity. *Opposite:* The zebra's disruptive coloring is so effective that in a herd such as this one at Busch Gardens, it's difficult to separate one animal from the next. *Following pages:* The "new zoo" combines animals from the same ecological setting in the same exhibit, such as this reticulated giraffe and these impalas, all from the African grasslands.

Although the elephant leads a precarious existence in the wild because of poaching, the animal is a common and generally long-lived fixture in most American zoos. *Opposite:* Rough disciplinary treatment, which some keepers say is the only way to keep captive elephants under control, continues to be debated by the zoo community and animal rights organizations.

As the human population boom continues, devouring ever more of the limited open space left on Earth, many more species will find themselves facing the same situation. Few knowledgeable observers will be surprised if elephants and rhinoceroses are completely gone from the wild by the year 2000. Today, American zoos are home to more Siberian tigers than the big cat's wild homeland, and there are no signs of a reversal.

Amazingly, such species may be the lucky ones. Because of the attention being given them, some of their kind may survive this period in which the Earth is experiencing the greatest loss of species since the sudden disappearance of the dinosaurs. An estimated six species are now vanishing every week. The most species-intensive habitat, the rain forest, is disappearing at the rate of about 100 acres per minute. Some people fear that zoos and zoo-like preserves may become the only places where this type of ecosystem can be found.

Zoos have responded well to their role as the modern Noah's ark. Breeding programs are under way for species that were only vaguely understood a few

Llamas are among the animals most commonly found in zoos. *Bottom:* The llama, one of the species often included in those parts of the zoo where humans and animals mingle, has gained a well-deserved reputation for spitting when disturbed. *Opposite:* Bactrian camels may no longer exist in the wild, except for those few that have escaped from captivity. An endangered species, it is nonetheless still used as a beast of burden by the native people of the Gobi desert.

The dromedary camel is native to Africa and Asia. Attempts to introduce it into the wild on other continents have been unsuccessful. *Below:* The endangered Bactrain has two humps, while the dromedary has just one. *Opposite:* The muskox was the species chosen as the U.S.'s gift to China in exchange for the famous giant pandas that became the star attractions at the National Zoo in Washington, D.C.

The cape buffalo has the largest horns of any animal and a mean disposition when threatened. These two factors have given the beast the reputation of being one of the most dangerous animals on the face of the Earth, although this cow and calf appear placid enough.

years ago. The many idiosyncrasies of each species are taken into account. Cheetahs, hearing others of their kind in their immediate vicinity, will not breed. Sable antelopes insist on complete privacy before breeding. Even the prolific lion must be in perfect health to mate successfully. The list goes on and on, with even more yet to learn.

Some species, on the other hand, need only the slightest encouragement. Tigers do phenomenally well breeding in captivity. In some years, the zoo-held population of the big cats has actually added a full 50 percent to its numbers.

For those species that have had a more difficult time making the adjustment, such as the giant panda, new methods are being developed. For example, in vitro fertilization, which involves the combining of egg and sperm outside the female's body followed by the implanting of the fertilized egg back into the female, has been successful in humans, as well as in many types of domestic livestock. Applications to zoo animals are under study, with the aim of helping

Preceding page: **This man-made mountain at the Denver Zoological Gardens closely simulates the dall sheep's natural, high country habitat.** *This page, top to bottom:* **In the wild, severe weather and food shortages would be the chief enemies of this bighorn lamb, although mountain lions, wolves, coyotes, bears, and eagles also would pose a threat. Desert bighorn sheep are among the native species that inhabit the Sonora Desert Museum, a regionally-oriented zoo in Tucson, Arizona. The sable antelope is one species that mates only in total privacy.**

Canines, like this pair of gray foxes, are often lackadaisical under the traditional bar-and-concrete zoo conditions. Given natural conditions, however, they can be quite active. *Below:* Fairy tales that include the villainous "big bad wolf" continue a long line of undeserved indignities that man has heaped upon the wolf. Time spent watching a pack in a zoo will present an entirely different picture of the animal.

those species that have shown difficulty in captive breeding, including some of our most endangered species.

In addition to the monumentally important task of getting as many species as possible into the next century, our zoos have a responsibility to educate the public. This, too, is a task of increased importance in today's shrinking world. Many of the new zoos concentrate their educational efforts on publicizing the dangers facing animals and their ecosystems.

For many millions of people, the zoo experience will be their only contact with exotic environments. Whatever concern for conservation they may have will be shaped, in large part, as they stroll among the enclosures.

Each animal, then, becomes an ambassador for its species, even for its entire ecosystem. The new display methods make the most of this by showing each animal in as natural an environment as possible, displaying the behaviors each would exhibit in the wild.

Not that the lazy lion, lounging about its ceramic-tiled cell, was any less deserving of protection. The king of beasts surrounded by a re-creation of its African homeland is nearly as lazy and does almost as much

Whether in the wild or in the zoo, the raccoon-like lesser panda spends most of the daylight hours curled up in a tree. *Right:* **The lesser panda naturally inhabits the rugged, bamboo-forested slopes of the Himalayas between 6,000 and 12,000 feet above sea level.**

lounging about. But the imagery created by the setting is entirely different, and helps zoo visitors to understand the relationship of the animal to the environment.

All of this is worlds away from the original zoos, which were collections of the oddest animals that could be found and captured as a demonstration of the power of humans over animals and the natural world.

No one is certain if it was the very first zoo, but Queen Hatshepsut of ancient Egypt maintained a zoo sometime around 1500 B.C. She is also credited with organizing the first animal-collecting expedition. Her hunters were sent out to scour the Red Sea region for leopards, wild cattle, and monkeys that would elevate her palace zoo above other contemporary menageries, which housed hares and wild cats.

The Chinese emperor Wen Wang developed his massive, 1,500-acre Garden of Intelligence about 500 years later. Other African, Indian, and Chinese rulers followed suit with their own small menageries over the next century.

Preceding page: **With its highly selective diet that is based primarily on bamboo, the giant panda is extremely susceptible to shortages of the plant.** *This page, top to bottom:* **The giant panda is commonly and incorrectly referred to as a bear, although it is not a member of the ursine family. The first giant panda (named Su-lin) to be brought out of China in modern times was exhibited at the Brookfield Zoo in Chicago in 1937. A popular zoo animal in the few locations that it is exhibited, the giant panda engages in a wide variety of human-like behaviors and movements.**

While brown bears vary greatly in size and coloring, there appear to be only two true subspecies: the grizzly and the Kodiak. *Below:* The brown bear remains the most widespread member of the ursine family. *Opposite:* The bear is strength incarnate, able to shatter thick saplings with a single swipe of its heavily clawed paw.

The smallest of all bears, the sun bear of southeast Asia may also be the world's rarest. It has been on the most endangered list since 1978.

Alaskan brown bears are quite at home in the water. During the salmon run, the big bears may each eat more than a dozen salmon in a given day. *Below:* These brown bear cubs began life weighing less than a pound. They may eventually increase their weight by 1,000 times or more.

These pages: The thick coat of the polar bear enables the animal to survive incredibly cold temperatures. Polar bears are able to swim more than 60 miles without rest. They propel themselves with their front paws and use their rear paws like rudders.

The tusks of the walrus are actually elongated canine teeth which extend as much as three feet. Like the tusks of the elephant, they are made of ivory. *Opposite:* The California sea lion spends most of its day basking in the sun. In the wild, it spends the nighttime hours feeding on fish and mollusks.

The kangaroo, a common resident of zoos throughout the world, is the most instantly recognizable representative of the strange fauna that has evolved on the isolated Australian continent. *Below:* Like its fellow marsupials, including the opossum of North America, the female kangaroo carries her offspring in an abdominal pouch throughout the first months of their lives. *Opposite:* The koala has one of the most restricted diets of any animal, eating only eucalyptus leaves that are at a certain stage of growth. Consequently, only a few zoos can sustain the animal.

Public zoos were a normal part of city life for ancient Greek citizens, who devoted a great deal of time to the study of the animal and plant life on display there. Private zoos were popular among the wealthy of ancient Rome, and the collection of animals maintained by Romans as a supply of bloody combatants for the Colosseum was on public display.

European zoos, like much of European life, were severely set back by the Dark Ages. But a few collections did persist. The menagerie that Henry I founded in the early 1100's continued in the Tower of London into the early 1880's. France's Philip VI had his own collection as early as 1333. And, as new interest in learning and exploration emerged at the end of the 1400's, so did a desire for zoos.

Although many of the emerging collections amounted to nothing more than a few poorly-kept bears and lions, they sprang up quickly over the next two centuries. Disgust at the terrible conditions of the menageries led to their replacement by larger collections living under better conditions, which developed into our first modern zoos.

This page, top to bottom: **Primates, such as these chimpanzees, are by nature active, inquisitive creatures but in the steel and concrete enclosures of traditional zoos they often turn these energies to abnormal behavior. In the "new zoo," they exhibit more natural behaviors, such as the group-grooming of these pygmy chimpanzees. A troop of apes seeks shelter together, just as they might in the wild.** *Opposite:* **In the past, the animal trade had a major impact on the chimpanzee population in the wild, but today zoos find all the chimps they need in domestic breeding programs.**

Preceding pages, left: The aptly-named proboscis monkey of Borneo sports one of the strangest noses in the animal kingdom. In some old males it is as long as seven inches. *Right:* Although the lowland gorilla is more numerous than the highly endangered mountain gorilla, no more than 20,000 remain today. *This page, above:* The first gorilla born in captivity arrived December 24, 1956, in Columbus, Ohio. The young female was not cared for by her mother and had to be raised by zookeepers. *Left:* Very few white gorillas have ever been recorded, either in captivity or in the wild. Part of the reason for this may be that in the wild a white ape would have very little chance of survival.

The natural range of the orangutan is shrinking at an alarming rate. The ape is now found wild only in Borneo and Sumatra. *Below:* In the wild, in past years, this mother orangutan might very well have been killed in order to capture her offspring for the animal trade.

Great apes placed in traditional cages frequently exhibit behaviors unknown in the wild.

Crocodiles may not be the most entertaining of zoo residents, but they offer a glimpse into Earth's distant past. The reptile existed, much in its present form, 300 million years ago. *Below:* "Yawning" is one of the few motions made by crocodiles that visitors to a zoo will witness, since crocodiles are naturally creatures of minimal activity.

Captive or wild, alligators spend much of their days basking in the sun. Until recently, the alligator was considered an endangered species. *Below:* The alligator is an extremely long-lived creature. Ages of more than 50 years are not uncommon in captivity.

The oldest of these zoos still in operation is the Schonbrunn Zoo in Vienna, Austria, which saw its first visitors in 1752. Other long-running zoos are the Madrid Zoo in Spain, which began in 1775, and the Paris Zoo, which was established in 1793. But it was the British who, in the late nineteenth century, coined the term "zoo" which is actually an abbreviated version of "zoological garden."

In the Americas, at least one large-scale zoo existed centuries before European "civilization" had anything comparable. In 1519, when the Spanish explorer Hernando Cortez invaded the lands of the Aztecs in today's Mexico, among the glories he found there was a zoo so large that the aviaries alone kept more than 300 zookeepers busy. But like many of the achievements of the advanced empire, this collection of mammals, birds, and reptiles was lost in the ensuing takeover by the Spanish.

The U.S. waited much longer for the development of its zoos, which today include some of the very best in the world.

The female ostrich lays the largest egg of any bird, but the incubation period (about 40 days) is of average length. *Left:* Many visitors to the zoo misidentify the emu as an ostrich. It is, however, quite a distinct species: the ostrich is the largest bird, while the emu ranks third.

The Philadelphia Zoological Society was chartered in 1859, but Civil War delays prevented the opening of the Philadelphia Zoo until 1874. By that time the Central Park Zoo (1864), the Buffalo Zoo in Buffalo, New York (1870), and the Lincoln Park Zoo in Chicago, Illinois (1874) were in operation. The Central Park Zoo already held a permanent collection of 581 specimens and was having success in breeding camels, lions, and leopards.

According to the International Zoo Yearbook, there are now more than a thousand zoos operating in over a hundred different countries, including everything from private collections of a few animals to expansive parks housing thousands of animals. No one knows how many small collections are not counted in that total.

The zoos of tomorrow will include far fewer small collections and menageries. Many municipally run zoos may fall by the wayside, unless they can find the means to update both their physical and operational statuses. The zoos that remain will be even less encyclopedic in their holdings, choosing instead to specialize in the life of a particular region or in a particular

This page, top to bottom: **Brightly colored parrots, such as these, continue to be pushed closer to the edge of extinction by hunters who are seeking their feathers, as well as the live birds for the pet trade. Natural habitats at many zoos have been designed to allow such beautiful birds to live in a nearly wild state. Raspy voiced macaws pair monogamously for life, with the female laying two large, white eggs each year in the cavity of a hollow tree.**

It is only in free flight that the full magnificence of the bald eagle can be appreciated. *Below:* The golden eagle is a very capable hunter in the wild, attacking prey as large as a deer. *Opposite:* Since beauty is in the eye of the beholder, even this king vulture can be admired for its bright coloring.

family of animal. Each one will house larger numbers of fewer species, with zoos as a whole thus accommodating viable breeding populations of many more species overall. Cooperation among zoos will reduce current exhibition pressures that lead to the overproduction of some species, such as tigers.

Zoo visitors may give up some of the "luxuries" associated with the old concrete and steel cages. A trip to the zoo will probably require active participation to steal a glimpse of some semi-wild creature as it roams through a dense jungle-like environment. Concepts beyond the simple fact that the polar bear is native to the Arctic, even troubling concepts of the limitations of our planet, will be presented.

In other words, zoos are becoming much more than a place for a casual stroll on a Sunday afternoon. Zoo animals are becoming much more than a spectacle for our temporary amusement. In a very real way, zoos hold a big part of our planet's future.

Like many white animals, the white peacock is a rare specimen. It would probably be unable to survive for long in the wild. *Left:* Lacking the vibrant blues, greens, and purples that make the average male peafowl a spectacle to behold, this white peacock nonetheless follows normal behaviors of display and courtship. *Opposite:* The peacock was among the first birds used in animal trade by humans. King Solomon reportedly kept the birds in his private menagerie and traded them for other exotic species. *Following pages:* Although today nearly every zoo or menagerie has a few peafowl, in Biblical times the birds were so rare and expensive that they cost about 2,000 times as much as any other bird.

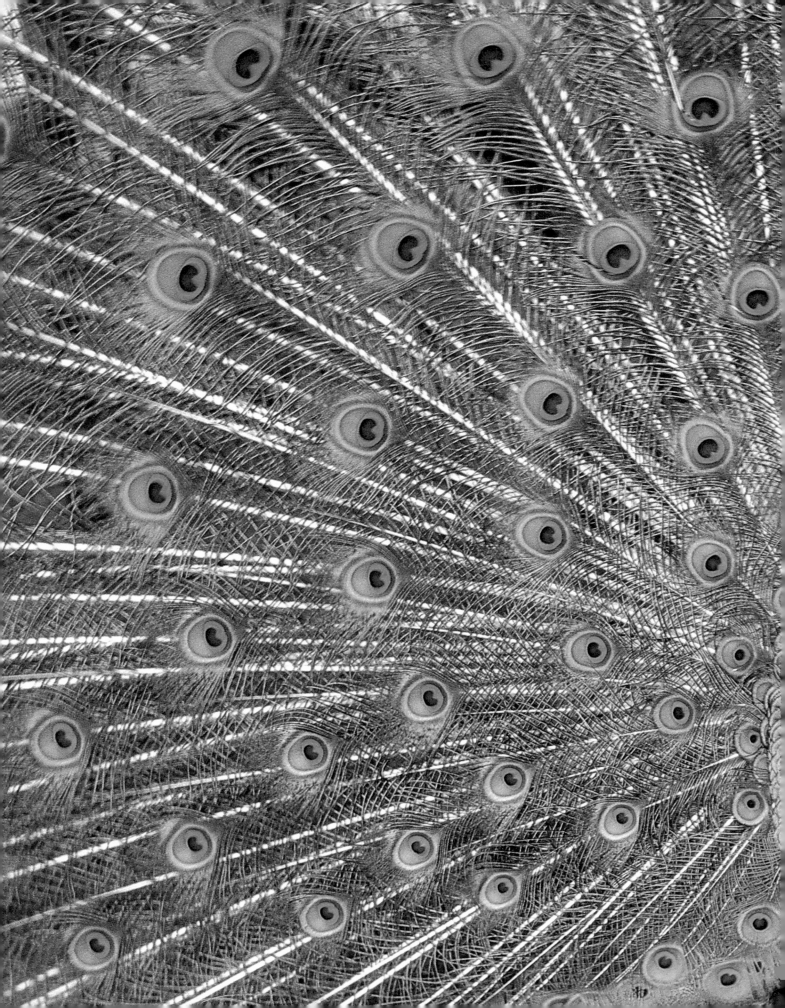

Index of Photography

All photographs courtesy of The Image Bank except
where indicated ★